AF270126

1 THESSALONIANS

NEW AMERICAN STANDARD BIBLE

SCRIPTURE STUDY NOTEBOOK

2 THESSALONIANS STARTS ON PAGE 37

NASB SCRIPTURE STUDY NOTEBOOK: 1 AND 2 THESSALONIANS
Copyright 2020 by Three Sixteen Publishing Inc.
Steadfast Bibles is a division of Three Sixteen Publishing Inc.
Requests for information should be directed to: info@316publishing.com

ISBN: 978-1-937212-74-2

Printed in China
26 25 24 23 22 21 20 / 1 2 3 4 5 6 7

EXPLANATION OF GENERAL FORMAT

Paragraphs are designated by bold face verse numbers or letters.

Personal Pronouns are capitalized when pertaining to Deity.

Brackets indicate words probably not in the original languages.

Italics are used in the text to indicate words which are not found in the original Hebrew, Aramaic, or Greek but implied by it.

Small caps in the New Testament are used in the text to indicate Old Testament quotations or obvious references to Old Testament texts. Variations of Old Testament wording are found in New Testament citations depending on whether the New Testament writer translated from a Hebrew text, used existing Greek or Aramaic translations, or paraphrased the material. It should be noted that modern rules for the indication of direct quotation were not used in biblical times; thus, the ancient writer would use exact quotations or references to quotation without specific indication of such.

An Asterisk (*) is used to mark verbs that are historical presents in the Greek which have been translated with an English past tense in order to conform to modern usage. The translators recognized that in some contexts the present tense seems more unexpected and unjustified to the English reader than a past tense would have been. But Greek authors frequently used the present tense for the sake of heightened vividness, thereby transporting their readers in imagination to the actual scene at the time of occurrence. However, the translators felt that it would be wise to change these historical presents to English past tenses.

1 Paul and Silvanus and Timothy,

To the church of the Thessalonians in God the Father and the Lord Jesus Christ: Grace to you and peace.

2 We give thanks to God always for all of you, making mention *of you* in our prayers;

3 constantly bearing in mind your work of faith and labor of love and steadfastness of hope in our Lord Jesus Christ in the presence of our God and Father,

4 knowing, brethren beloved by God, *His* choice of you;

5 for our gospel did not come to you in word only, but also in power and in the Holy Spirit and with full conviction; just as you know what kind of men we proved to be among you for your sake.

6 You also became imitators of us and of the Lord, having received the word in much tribulation with the joy of the Holy Spirit,

7 so that you became an example to all the believers in Macedonia and in Achaia.

8 For the word of the Lord has sounded forth from you, not only in Macedonia and Achaia, but also in every place your faith toward God has gone forth, so that we have no need to say anything.

9 For they themselves report about us what kind of a reception we had with you, and how you turned to God from idols to serve a living and true God,

10 and to wait for His Son from heaven, whom He raised from the dead, *that is* Jesus, who rescues us from the wrath to come.

2 For you yourselves know, brethren, that our coming to you was not in vain,

2 but after we had already suffered and been mistreated in Philippi, as you know, we had the boldness in our God to speak to you the gospel of God amid much opposition.

3 For our exhortation does not *come* from error or impurity or by way of deceit;

4 but just as we have been approved by God to be entrusted with the gospel, so we speak, not as pleasing men, but God who examines our hearts.

5 For we never came with flattering speech, as you know, nor with a pretext for greed—God is witness—

6 nor did we seek glory from men, either from you or from others, even though as apostles of Christ we might have asserted our authority.

7 But we proved to be gentle among you, as a nursing *mother* tenderly cares for her own children.

8 Having so fond an affection for you, we were well-pleased to impart to you not only the gospel of God but also our own lives, because you had become very dear to us.

9 For you recall, brethren, our labor and hardship, *how* working night and day so as not to be a burden to any of you, we proclaimed to you the gospel of God.

10 You are witnesses, and *so is* God, how devoutly and uprightly and blamelessly we behaved toward you believers;

11 just as you know how we *were* exhorting and encouraging and imploring each one of you as a father *would* his own children,

12 so that you would walk in a manner worthy of the God who calls you into His own kingdom and glory.

13 For this reason we also constantly thank God that when you received the word of God which you heard from us, you accepted *it* not *as* the word of men, but *for* what it really is, the word of God, which also performs its work in you who believe.

14 For you, brethren, became imitators of the churches of God in Christ Jesus that are in Judea, for you also endured the same sufferings at the hands of your own countrymen, even as they *did* from the Jews,

15 who both killed the Lord Jesus and the prophets, and drove us out. They are not pleasing to God, but hostile to all men,

16 hindering us from speaking to the Gentiles so that they may be saved; with the result that they always fill up the measure of their sins. But wrath has come upon them to the utmost.

17 But we, brethren, having been taken away from you for a short while—in person, not in spirit—were all the more eager with great desire to see your face.

18 For we wanted to come to you—I, Paul, more than once—and *yet* Satan hindered us.

19 For who is our hope or joy or crown of exultation? Is it not even you, in the presence of our Lord Jesus at His coming?

20 For you are our glory and joy.

3 Therefore when we could endure *it* no longer, we thought it best to be left behind at Athens alone,

2 and we sent Timothy, our brother and God's fellow worker in the gospel of Christ, to strengthen and encourage you as to your faith,

3 so that no one would be disturbed by these afflictions; for you yourselves know that we have been destined for this.

4 For indeed when we were with you, we *kept* telling you in advance that we were going to suffer affliction; and so it came to pass, as you know.

5 For this reason, when I could endure *it* no longer, I also sent to find out about your faith, for fear that the tempter might have tempted you, and our labor would be in vain.

6 But now that Timothy has come to us from you, and has brought us good news of your faith and love, and that you always think kindly of us, longing to see us just as we also long to see you,

7 for this reason, brethren, in all our distress and affliction we were comforted about you through your faith;

8 for now we *really* live, if you stand firm in the Lord.

9 For what thanks can we render to God for you in return for all the joy with which we rejoice before our God on your account,

10 as we night and day keep praying most earnestly that we may see your face, and may complete what is lacking in your faith?

11 Now may our God and Father Himself and Jesus our Lord direct our way to you;

12 and may the Lord cause you to increase and abound in love for one another, and for all people, just as we also *do* for you;

13 so that He may establish your hearts without blame in holiness before our God and Father at the coming of our Lord Jesus with all His saints.

4 Finally then, brethren, we request and exhort you in the Lord Jesus, that as you received from us *instruction* as to how you ought to walk and please God (just as you actually do walk), that you excel still more.

2 For you know what commandments we gave you by *the authority of* the Lord Jesus.

3 For this is the will of God, your sanctification; *that is,* that you abstain from sexual immorality;

4 that each of you know how to possess his own vessel in sanctification and honor,

5 not in lustful passion, like the Gentiles who do not know God;

6 *and* that no man transgress and defraud his brother in the matter because the Lord is *the* avenger in all these things, just as we also told you before and solemnly warned *you.*

7 For God has not called us for the purpose of impurity, but in sanctification.

8 So, he who rejects *this* is not rejecting man but the God who gives His Holy Spirit to you.

9 Now as to the love of the brethren, you have no need for *anyone* to write to you, for you yourselves are taught by God to love one another;

10 for indeed you do practice it toward all the brethren who are in all Macedonia. But we urge you, brethren, to excel still more,

11 and to make it your ambition to lead a quiet life and attend to your own business and work with your hands, just as we commanded you,

12 so that you will behave properly toward outsiders and not be in any need.

13 But we do not want you to be uninformed, brethren, about those who are asleep, so that you will not grieve as do the rest who have no hope.

14 For if we believe that Jesus died and rose again, even so God will bring with Him those who have fallen asleep in Jesus.

15 For this we say to you by the word of the Lord, that we who are alive and remain until the coming of the Lord, will not precede those who have fallen asleep.

16 For the Lord Himself will descend from heaven with a shout, with the voice of *the* archangel and with the trumpet of God, and the dead in Christ will rise first.

17 Then we who are alive and remain will be caught up together with them in the clouds to meet the Lord in the air, and so we shall always be with the Lord.

18 Therefore comfort one another with these words.

5 Now as to the times and the epochs, brethren, you have no need of anything to be written to you.

2 For you yourselves know full well that the day of the Lord will come just like a thief in the night.

3 While they are saying, "Peace and safety!" then destruction will come upon them suddenly like labor pains upon a woman with child, and they will not escape.

4 But you, brethren, are not in darkness, that the day would overtake you like a thief;

5 for you are all sons of light and sons of day. We are not of night nor of darkness;

6 so then let us not sleep as others do, but let us be alert and sober.

7 For those who sleep do their sleeping at night, and those who get drunk get drunk at night.

8 But since we are of *the* day, let us be sober, having put on the breastplate of faith and love, and as a helmet, the hope of salvation.

9 For God has not destined us for wrath, but for obtaining salvation through our Lord Jesus Christ,

10 who died for us, so that whether we are awake or asleep, we will live together with Him.

11 Therefore encourage one another and build up one another, just as you also are doing.

12 But we request of you, brethren, that you appreciate those who diligently labor among you, and have charge over you in the Lord and give you instruction,

13 and that you esteem them very highly in love because of their work. Live in peace with one another.

14 We urge you, brethren, admonish the unruly, encourage the fainthearted, help the weak, be patient with everyone.

15 See that no one repays another with evil for evil, but always seek after that which is good for one another and for all people.

16 Rejoice always;

17 pray without ceasing;

18 in everything give thanks; for this is God's will for you in Christ Jesus.

19 Do not quench the Spirit;

20 do not despise prophetic utterances.

21 But examine everything *carefully;* hold fast to that which is good;

22 abstain from every form of evil.

23 Now may the God of peace Himself sanctify you entirely;
and may your spirit and soul and body be preserved complete,
without blame at the coming of our Lord Jesus Christ.

24 Faithful is He who calls you, and He also will bring it to pass.

25 Brethren, pray for us.

26 Greet all the brethren with a holy kiss.

27 I adjure you by the Lord to have this letter read to all
the brethren.

28 The grace of our Lord Jesus Christ be with you.

2 THESSALONIANS

NEW AMERICAN STANDARD BIBLE

SCRIPTURE STUDY NOTEBOOK

1 Paul and Silvanus and Timothy,

To the church of the Thessalonians in God our Father and the Lord Jesus Christ:

2 Grace to you and peace from God the Father and the Lord Jesus Christ.

3 We ought always to give thanks to God for you, brethren, as is *only* fitting, because your faith is greatly enlarged, and the love of each one of you toward one another grows *ever* greater;

4 therefore, we ourselves speak proudly of you among the churches of God for your perseverance and faith in the midst of all your persecutions and afflictions which you endure.

5 *This is* a plain indication of God's righteous judgment so that you will be considered worthy of the kingdom of God, for which indeed you are suffering.

6 For after all it is *only* just for God to repay with affliction those who
   afflict you,

7 and *to give* relief to you who are afflicted and to us as well when
   the Lord Jesus will be revealed from heaven with His mighty angels
   in flaming fire,

8 dealing out retribution to those who do not know God and to those
   who do not obey the gospel of our Lord Jesus.

9 These will pay the penalty of eternal destruction, away from the
   presence of the Lord and from the glory of His power,

10 when He comes to be glorified in His saints on that day, and to be
   marveled at among all who have believed—for our testimony to
   you was believed.

11 To this end also we pray for you always, that our God will count you
   worthy of your calling, and fulfill every desire for goodness and the
   work of faith with power,

12 so that the name of our Lord Jesus will be glorified in you,
   and you in Him, according to the grace of our God and *the*
   Lord Jesus Christ.

2 Now we request you, brethren, with regard to the coming of our Lord Jesus Christ and our gathering together to Him,

2 that you not be quickly shaken from your composure or be disturbed either by a spirit or a message or a letter as if from us, to the effect that the day of the Lord has come.

3 Let no one in any way deceive you, for *it will not come* unless the apostasy comes first, and the man of lawlessness is revealed, the son of destruction,

4 who opposes and exalts himself above every so-called god or object of worship, so that he takes his seat in the temple of God, displaying himself as being God.

5 Do you not remember that while I was still with you, I was telling you these things?

6   And you know what restrains him now, so that in his time he will
be revealed.

7   For the mystery of lawlessness is already at work; only he who now
restrains *will do so* until he is taken out of the way.

8   Then that lawless one will be revealed whom the Lord will slay with
the breath of His mouth and bring to an end by the appearance of
His coming;

9   *that is,* the one whose coming is in accord with the activity of
Satan, with all power and signs and false wonders,

10   and with all the deception of wickedness for those who perish,
because they did not receive the love of the truth so as to be saved.

11   For this reason God will send upon them a deluding influence so
that they will believe what is false,

12   in order that they all may be judged who did not believe the truth,
but took pleasure in wickedness.

13 But we should always give thanks to God for you, brethren beloved by the Lord, because God has chosen you from the beginning for salvation through sanctification by the Spirit and faith in the truth.

14 It was for this He called you through our gospel, that you may gain the glory of our Lord Jesus Christ.

15 So then, brethren, stand firm and hold to the traditions which you were taught, whether by word *of mouth* or by letter from us.

16 Now may our Lord Jesus Christ Himself and God our Father, who has loved us and given us eternal comfort and good hope by grace,

17 comfort and strengthen your hearts in every good work and word.

3 Finally, brethren, pray for us that the word of the Lord will spread rapidly and be glorified, just as *it did* also with you;

2   and that we will be rescued from perverse and evil men; for not all have faith.

3   But the Lord is faithful, and He will strengthen and protect you from the evil *one.*

4   We have confidence in the Lord concerning you, that you are doing and will *continue to* do what we command.

5   May the Lord direct your hearts into the love of God and into the steadfastness of Christ.

6 Now we command you, brethren, in the name of our Lord Jesus Christ, that you keep away from every brother who leads an unruly life and not according to the tradition which you received from us.

7 For you yourselves know how you ought to follow our example, because we did not act in an undisciplined manner among you,

8 nor did we eat anyone's bread without paying for it, but with labor and hardship we *kept* working night and day so that we would not be a burden to any of you;

9 not because we do not have the right *to this,* but in order to offer ourselves as a model for you, so that you would follow our example.

10 For even when we were with you, we used to give you this order: if anyone is not willing to work, then he is not to eat, either.

11 For we hear that some among you are leading an undisciplined life, doing no work at all, but acting like busybodies.

12 Now such persons we command and exhort in the Lord Jesus Christ to work in quiet fashion and eat their own bread.

13 But as for you, brethren, do not grow weary of doing good.

14 If anyone does not obey our instruction in this letter, take special note of that person and do not associate with him, so that he will be put to shame.

15 *Yet* do not regard him as an enemy, but admonish him as a brother.

16 Now may the Lord of peace Himself continually grant you peace in every circumstance. The Lord be with you all!

17 I, Paul, write this greeting with my own hand, and this is a distinguishing mark in every letter; this is the way I write.

18 The grace of our Lord Jesus Christ be with you all.